Brigitte Sedlaczek

PETRA
Art and Legend

Distributed by:
Mazen Al Harris Books
Tel: 643139 - 625424
Amman

Published by:
MP Graphic Formula
Rome, Italy
1997

*On the following page, the Al-Khasneh (Treasury)
seen from the Siq, from a drawing by David Roberts.*

3

Petra

In enchanting mountain scenery in southern Jordan, surrounded by gorges and rock, there lies a city which is unique in the world - Petra. It is situated at an altitude of 950 m, about 260 km south of Amman and 30 km north-west of the village of Ma'an in the Wadi Musa. Its name means "rock", from the Greek translation of the Hebrew name Selah. It is mentioned in the Bible as the capital of the Kingdom of Edom. The Edomites, who were a Semitic people, settled in the area between the Dead Sea and the Gulf of Aqaba in around the 13th century BC, during the early Iron Age. Shortly afterwards the area was occupied by the Nabataeans, a group of nomadic Arabs who originated in northern Arabia. They are mentioned for the first time in the year 647 BC, when the Assyrian King Ashurbanipal spoke of them as his enemies, although they had not yet occupied Petra.

It was around 300 BC when they founded, in what is now modern Jordan, their peculiar "caravan kingdom".

At first, the Nabataeans were principally raiders of caravans, but soon they were in a position to control the traffic between neighbouring states. They organised guard posts, controlled wells and imposed tolls on the roads. Their trade, carried out by means of caravans of camels along the "Incense Road" reached the ports of Gaza and Aqaba and extended right out to the Far East. They principally traded in animals, spices, incense, myrrh, iron, copper, cloth, sugar, medicines, gold and ivory, and they also mined bitumen (asphalt) from the Red Sea to be sold in Egypt where it was used in the mummification process. The Nabataeans also created large irrigation systems, using a very advanced and ingenious system of channels and dams which guaranteed water supplies throughout the land.

It is likely that Petra became the Nabataean capital at the height of its fortune. Under the reign of Harith III (87-62 BC),

Nabataean territory reached its greatest expansion, with even the Syrian cities of Damascus and Bozrah falling under its influence. It was an extraordinary state - without any real borders, no taxes and very few slaves, and also, it seems, very little social unrest. It was therefore a very peaceful state whose main preoccupation was the collection of commercial duties. The Nabataeans were also skilled in the art of diplomacy, preferring this as a method of placating military provocations.

One example of this was when they were attacked by the Diadochus Antigonus (one of the successors of Alexander the Great). The historian Strabo recounts how the Nabataeans reacted in a most unusual way - by taking refuge in the rocky heights of the surrounding mountains and offering their attackers generous gifts! Something similar occurred with the Romans who tried on two occasions, in 63 and 25 BC, to conquer the territory of the Nabataeans, who preferred to negotiate rather than fight. But from the year 106 AD, when the Romans under Trajan declared the northern end of the peninsula to be part of their province of Arabia and intensified maritime traffic on the Red Sea, the Nabataeans found themselves unable to keep up this strategy. They did manage to hold on to their monopoly, however, right up to the 3rd century AD, at which stage domination of the trade routes fell into the hands of Palmyra.

In the Byzantine age, Petra became a bishopric but was hit badly by an earthquake in the 6th century and when Palestine fell to the forces of Islam in the 7th century, the once powerful trade empire of the Nabataeans collapsed and fell into oblivion.

A few centuries later, around the year 1100, the Crusaders arrived at Petra and built a fort there. Sultan Baybars also visited Petra on the 8th April 1276, while he was on his way from Cairo to Kerak.

The Roman arch recorded in an old print, drawn by Léon De Laborde.

From then on, Petra grew ever less important and no more was heard of it, except for its inhabitants, the Bedouins, who through fear of foreign influences, jealously guarded the city from the eyes of strangers.

It was only by chance that in the summer of 1812 a westerner, Johann Ludwig Burckhardt, from Switzerland, who was passing through the region, managed to trick the locals into letting him get a glimpse of some of the ruins. After him, though, there followed other explorers from England, France and Germany who brought back drawings of the city, which later proved very useful in the graphic reconstruction of the monuments.

The real excavation work, however, did not begin until 1929 under the aegis of G. and A. Horsfield, with financing from Lord Melchett's Petra Exploration Fund, which also funded subsequent excavations from 1932 to 1936 together with the Jordanian government.

The first certain date in Nabataean history is 312 BC. It concerns the wars of the Diadochi, the generals who succeeded Alexander the Great. The first mention of the Nabataeans in history is from the pen of Diodorus Siculus, in his history of the world written in the time of Caesar. His source was a certain Jeronymus of Cardia, who was a high official in the government of the Diadochus Antigonus Monophthalmos and was for some time responsible for the extraction of bitumen from the Dead Sea.

As a result of his activities, he would have known the Nabataeans well, as it was they who extracted the bitumen.

Based on the writings of various ancient authors and on around 3,000 Nabataean inscriptions, we are now able to put together the story of this Arabic nation. The last mention of the Nabataeans comes on an inscription dated 328 AD.

Modern Arabic script has its origins in Nabataean, a fact which is worthy of note.

The Wadi Musa characterises Petra's topography and its urban development. Petra can be divided into various parts. For prehistoric sites, one very important area is Al-Baidha, which is 1 km south-west of As-Siq al-Barid, north of the town centre. Then there are the Nabataean monuments, tombs and temples, which are spread all over the area and include a piece of the town wall. The real centre of the Nabataean lower city dates from Roman times and provides such examples as the Cardo Maximus, the Monumental Gate, the Temenos, the baths, the Temple of the Winged Lions, and the Qasr al-Bint. North of the Temple of Winged Lions, excavations have been in progress since 1990 on a Christian basilica with three naves and floor mosaics. This work, financed by the American Center of Oriental Research, has already produced sensational results in the discovery of late ancient historical or ecclesiastical scrolls.

The Nabataean capital, Petra, with its multicoloured monuments carved from the mountainous region's sandstone, is an enchanting match of nature and culture. The last stretch of the "Incense Road" from southern Arabia, which passes through the Wadi Rum, even served as the backdrop in the classic film "Lawrence of Arabia".

To reach the city in its solemn solitude in the mountains, you must cross a concentration of rocky debris churned up by the rare but turbulent waters of the Wadi Musa, the Valley of Moses. Tradition has it that Moses produced water from the rock face by striking it with his staff, and in his honour a small mosque with three domes was erected to Moses, who is also venerated by Muslims, to recall the religious origins of the spring.

The importance of Wadi Musa is seen in the fertile land which spreads down in terraces from the top of the valley to the bottom. In ancient times, there was even an aqueduct several kilometres long which brought water right to the centre of the town.

Archaeological digs have unearthed an

Above, view of a Bedouin camp from a drawing by David Roberts.

Edomite settlement at Tawilan, half an hour on foot north-west of Ain Musa, the site of the spring.

From here there is a wonderful view of the Petran countryside. In the distance rises Jabal Harun, the highest point.

The horizon is dotted with small dark or yellowish-red rocky peaks, worn smooth by the wind. Jabal Harun and its stony surroundings are home to the site of this ancient city.

Once past the entrance and the Visitors' Centre, you pass along a white road which runs beside the bed of the Musa river, straight into one's first contact with Nabataean architecture, the three block tombs of the Bab es-Siq. As a result of archaeological studies in the winter of 1978-79, we now presume, even in the absence of bones or burial items, that these were sepulchral monuments comparable, in style, to a Nabataean tomb in the Syrian town of Suweida. Although this city lies in rubble, it has passed down to us through the drawings of the Conte de Vogué.

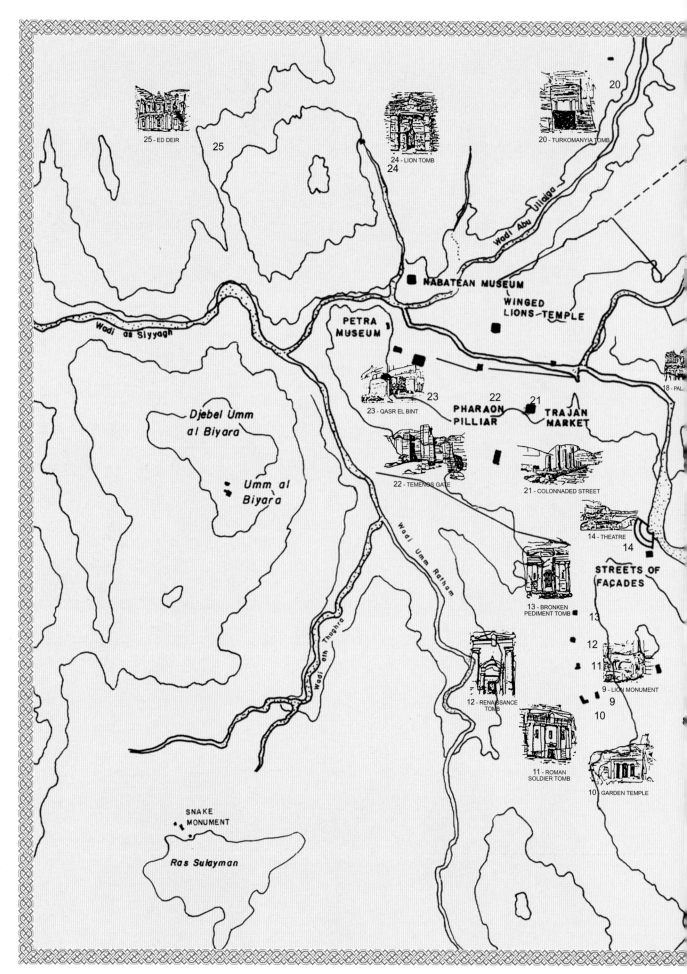

25 - ED DEIR

25

24 - LION TOMB

24

20 - TURKOMANYIA TOMB

20

NABATEAN MUSEUM

WINGED LIONS-TEMPLE

Wadi Abu Ullaiqa

PETRA MUSEUM

Wadi as Siyyagh

Djebel Umm al Biyara

Umm al Biyara

23 - QASR EL BINT

23

PHARAON PILLIAR

22

22 - TEMENOS GATE

21

TRAJAN MARKET

21 - COLONNADED STREET

18 - PAL

Wadi Umm Ratham

Wadi ath Thughra

14 - THEATRE

14

STREETS OF FAÇADES

13 - BRONKEN PEDIMENT TOMB

13

12

12 - RENAISSANCE TOMB

11

9 - LION MONUMENT

9

10

11 - ROMAN SOLDIER TOMB

10 - GARDEN TEMPLE

SNAKE MONUMENT

Ras Sulayman

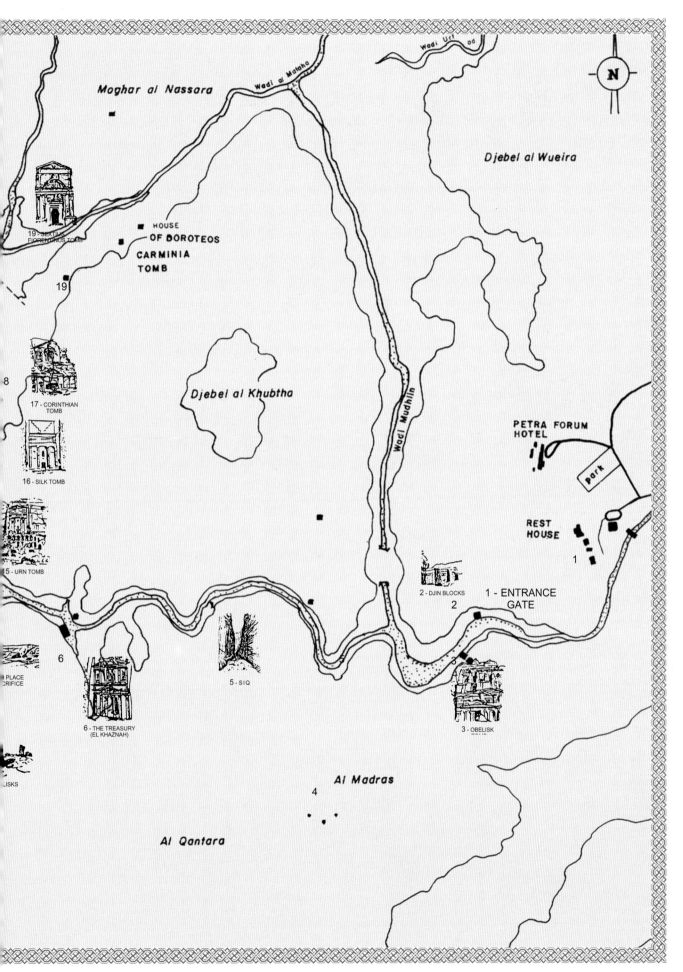

Moghar al Nassara

Wadi al Mataha

Wadi Urf ad

Djebel al Wueira

19 - SEXTIUS
FIORENTINUS TOMB

HOUSE
OF DOROTEOS
CARMINIA
TOMB

19

8

17 - CORINTHIAN
TOMB

Djebel al Khubtha

16 - SILK TOMB

Wadi Mudhlim

PETRA FORUM
HOTEL

Park

15 - URN TOMB

REST
HOUSE

1

2 - DJIN BLOCKS

1 - ENTRANCE
GATE

2

6

PLACE
CRIFICE

3

5 - SIQ

6 - THE TREASURY
(EL KHAZNAH)

3 - OBELISK

LISKS

4

Al Madras

Al Qantara

The Pioneers of Petra

In the summer of 1812, a young Swiss explorer dressed as a Bedouin was travelling from Aleppo to Cairo. He had been studying Arabic for two years in Syria, along with Islamic law and theology, and had been engaged by an English company to study the source of the Niger river in Africa.

His name was Johann Ludwig Burckhardt, born in Lausanne, Switzerland on the 24th November 1784. He studied at Leipzig and Göttingen Universities in Germany and later, moved to England in 1806.

He is not, however, remembered as an explorer of darkest Africa, but for the re-discovery of the ancient Jordanian city of Petra. In fact, he never reached his African destination as he died of dysentery in Cairo on the 17th October 1817.

In the summer of 1812, Burckhardt, disguised as "Sheikh Ibrahim", wearing Arab clothes and speaking Arabic, was riding across the plain of Edom, which lies east and south-east of the Dead Sea, when he learned from his Bedouin companions of an ancient ruined city hidden in the remote mountains which immediately sparked his interest. It was only through trickery that he was able to persuade them to accompany him to the spot. He told them of a vow he had made to visit the tomb of Harun (Aaron, the brother of Moses) which he knew to be in the area. As Harun is much venerated in Islam, the Bedouin could hardly deny him this request. So it was that on the 22nd

August 1812, Burckhardt came through the Siq, the first European in our age to have done so, and reached the foot of Jabal Harun, where he sacrificed a goat. Despite the close attentions of the Bedouins, Burckhardt was able, in just a couple of hours, to make the first sketches of the ancient city and the "Treasury of the Pharaoh" (Al-Khasneh). He was aware that he had probably just discovered the Nabataean capital as he was well versed in the Bible and later wrote in his diary "it is probable that the ruins in Wadi Musa are of the ancient city of Petra". Even before the posthumous publication of his diaries in 1822, the story of the discovery of Petra spread, particularly in England and so, in May 1818, two English captains in the Royal Navy, C.L. Irby and J. Mangles, retraced Burckhardt's steps to visit the Nabataean city. They were the first to climb Jabal Harun and see the facade of the ed-Deir. Then in 1828 the French count, Léon de Laborde together with his artist Linant, arrived at Petra. It is thanks to them that today we have so many interesting lithographs of the ruins, as well as a new map of the city. They were later followed by numerous other scholars from Germany and America, but it was not until 1929 that the real excavation work on the city began.

The first modern visitors from the West trying to discover Petra used to camouflage themselves as Arabs in order to overcome the reluctance of the local Bedouins who did not want strangers in their city. In these photos, we can see Burckhardt (left) and De Laborde (this page) in Arab clothing.

Some Useful Information

- Petra is 262 km from Amman along the Desert Highway, 133 km from Aqaba, and 328 km from Jerusalem. There are regular bus, minibus and shared taxi services every day, connecting Petra to Amman and Aqaba.
- On excursions, always bring suncream, a sunhat and sunglasses during the hot season. Wear comfortable, sensible shoes suitable for a stony, sandy terrain. A first-aid kit and a torch will also be handy.
- The distance from the entrance to the lower city is about 3 km (half an hour's walk). There is an entrance fee.
- It is possible to pass through the Siq, a narrow gorge about 1 km long, either on foot or in a small cart for two (plus the driver).

- The el-Khasneh (Treasury) is in full sunlight around 11 o'clock.
- The Royal Tombs are well lit in the afternoons. You will need an hour to see them.
- Excursions to the High Place of Sacrifice on the Attouf Ridge are physically strenuous. It is best to visit them in the early morning, remembering you will need 2/3 hours there and back.
- Excursions to the ed-Deir (Monastery) are very tiring. The best light is found from the early afternoon to sundown. Allow for 3 hours there and back.

Before Reaching The Siq

There are many hidden monuments in Petra. For example, near the three block tombs, there are two large tombs carved into the sides of small gorges off to the side of the road. On the left towards the south, but before one reaches the Obelisk Tomb and the Bab el-Siq Triclinium, there is a large burial chamber, decorated with simple but very interesting motifs - beside a 50 cm long horse with a bethel on its back, there are two snakes, each approximately 1.5 m long, who are attacking a quadruped. According to the scientist F. Zayadine, the snake functions as a guard for tombs in Hellenistic and Roman symbology.

The Nabataeans venerated the "Jinns", large stone blocks, at times with carvings, as they were held to house the spirits of the dead.

The Obelisk Tomb and the Bab es-Siq Triclinium

About 500 m after the entrance on the left, the facades of two tombs appear, one on top of the other: The upper tomb is called the "Tomb of the Obelisks", the lower "The Bab es-Siq Triclinium". The Tomb of the Obelisks is crowned by four pyramidal pillars and has a Græco-Nabataean inscription from the period of the reign of Malik II (40-70 AD) which reads "This monument was erected by Abd Manku ... for himself, his descendants and their two descendants ..." The style of this tomb is visibly influenced by Egyptian architecture. The city of Alexandria in Egypt, in fact, was also an important centre for the cult of the god Dhushara.

The Bab es-Siq Triclinium was a place of meetings and commemorations and is held to date from the end of the 1st century AD, during the reign of the last Nabataean king, Rabbel II (70-106 AD).

The Siq

Just after crossing the small dam is the entrance to the Siq. In 1916-17, the "German-Turkish Command for the Protection of Monuments" reported that the "Wadi es-Siq, dry until now, was being inundated by torrential waters" after "only half an hour of rain".

More recently, a catastrophic flood caused the death of a number of people in the Siq during a storm.

Of disastrous floods of the past, that of 1895 is particularly well-remembered as it swept away the arch which at that time existed at the entrance to the Siq. We know what the arch was like thanks to the drawings by Laborde and Roberts from around 1860, and traces of the base remain to this day. This narrow ravine which leads to the lower city is one kilometre long and at times only two metres wide. The sides of the gorge are almost 100 m high.

The route follows the old river bed as it twists and turns along. Along the left-hand wall at a height of about 2 metres, there used to run an aqueduct which later turns right and continues along a system of clay pipes.

Only a few traces remain of the limestone blocks which once paved the ancient road. Along the way one encounters many votive niches and bas-reliefs, witness to the strong religious beliefs of the Nabataeans. It is also possible to see a badly-damaged image of a god, resting on two lions. A Greek inscription cites the donor as one Sabinus. As they walk along the Siq, visitors are usually struck by its extraordinary nature, by the fascinating multiplicity of forms and colours, with tones ranging from grey, sometimes dark, sometimes metallic, to pale brown and even to a bright rust, with shades of yellow, blue and green.

Almost at the end of the Siq, it narrows for the last time and the tops of the ravine's sides seem to touch. Suddenly, around a bend, there appears the shape of a building.

Along the Siq, a narrow corridor between towering walls, you can see votive niches, bas-reliefs and Jinn Blocks.

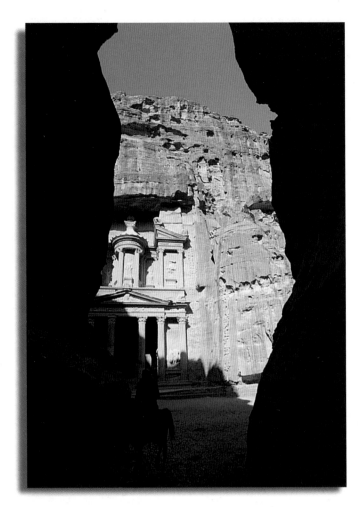

The Al-Khasneh (The Treasury)

Arriving from the Siq, you pass from the shade of the gorge into the splendour of an open place about 250m long by 70m wide, surrounded by rocky walls. In front of you lies Petra's most interesting monument - the reddish facade of the al-Khasneh Farun, the so-called Treasury of the Pharaoh.

This natural spectacle, combined with the work of man, generally produces an indescribable emotion in the heart of visitors. Archaeologists M. Linder and A. Negev hold this to be the most beautiful rock wall in the world, and is without doubt a milestone in Nabataean culture.

In the early dawn light the ferrous sandstone walls shine with a reddish colour. The name normally used for this monument, Al-Khasneh or Al-Khasneh Farun, means "the house of the treasure of the Pharaoh" and tradition states that the pharaoh hid some gold in the upper part of the monument. The inhabitants of the region today call it El-Jarra, which means "urn", and in fact the urn which crowns the tholos at the centre of the building, is riddled with bullet-holes from the Bedouins trying to get at the gold. The whole monument is massive - from the base to the urn it is almost 40 metres high and 28 metres wide. The urn itself is 3.5 m high. From an architectural point of view, this building, carved out of the rock, is an extraordinary piece of work.

The Treasury is carved on two distinct levels. In the lower part, a double row of columns outlines a portico which is entirely carved from solid rock. The central room is reached through a doorway. This room would have housed the body of some Nabataean or Roman personage. On the outer wall of the lower level there are high-relief carvings in the spaces between the two outer columns on each side of the facade. The carvings, which rest on a base, both show a man beside a horse, and are presumed to represent spirits who accompany the souls of the dead.

The upper level is divided into two sections with a central tholos, a type of cylindrical temple with columns which support a conical peristyle (roof). The famous urn rests on this roof.

In the centre of the tholos there is a goddess holding a cornucopia in her left arm. The goddess may be Isis or Tyche.

Between the columns to the side of the tholos there are some female figures, possibly amazons, who each hold an axe over their heads.

The niches behind the tholos contain figures of Victory and all the carvings rest on bases. The broken pediments of the niches are decorated on their lateral acroters with eagles, now in a very poor state.

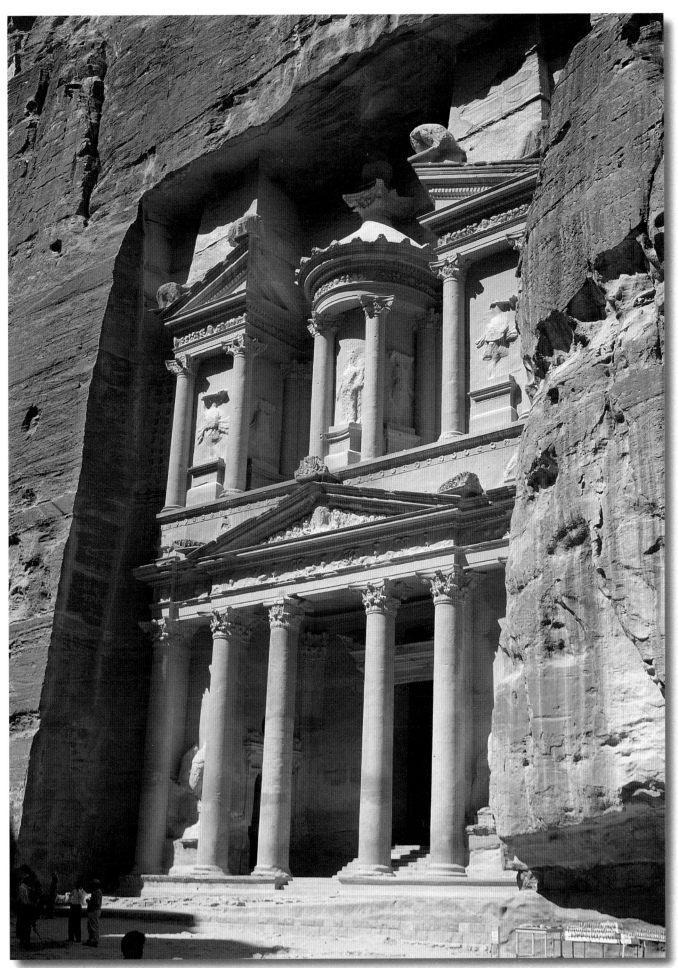

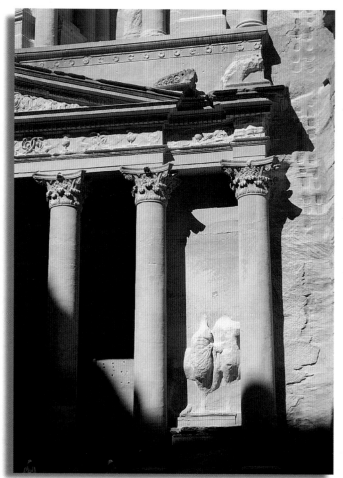

On this page, the tholos situated on the upper part of the Al-Khasneh facade, with some details.

On the previous page, some of the wonderful facades of tombs along the outer Siq.

The Street of Facades

After the emotions of the Al-Khasneh, the other facades along the Siq as it works its way towards the town centre seem of minor importance, but they are not. Along these rocky walls, countless splendid tombs stand out, and whole streets of tombs leave us a strong image of the Theatre Necropolis.

The Theatre

The theatre, which is situated in the lower city, merits special attention. When the archaeologist Philip C. Hammon was carrying out excavation work in the theatre in 1961/62, with financial assistance from the Jordanian Antiquities Office, the stage, the orchestra, the roofed side passages and part of the seating area, were all still underground. Today we know that on the 40 rows of stone steps, between 7,000 and 8,000 people could have been accommodated. This contrasts with the original estimates from the last century by Burckhardt and Robinson, which claimed a capacity of 3,000 to 4,000. The seating area was carved completely out of the solid rock of the mountain and followed the typical semi-circular Roman orchestral plan. The first building seems to have been during the Nabataean period with subsequent enlargements by the Romans, who brought it to its present size, damaging many of the burial chambers behind in the process.

Until 1960 the Theatre was considered to be a Roman construction, from the period following the annexation of Nabataea, but Hammond's most recent studies have seemed to confirm that it was originally built between 4 BC (the year of the death of Herod the Great) and 27 AD, during the reign of King Harith IV (9 BC - 40 AD). The theatre would have been in use for about half a century, only to fall into ruin until such times as the Romans, after 106 AD, restored its splendour. It is claimed that the theatre served as a reservoir during the Byzantine period.

Its definitive decline may well be connected to the earthquake of 19th May 365 AD.

Architectural Styles of the Facades
of Petra
(after I. Browning : Petra)

Denomination: Rectilinear
Dates: Archaic
Examples: The Siq tabernacles
The Street of Facades

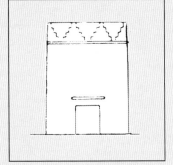

Denomination: Assyrian
Phase: I
Dates: 3rd, 2nd and 1st centuries BC
Characteristics: One single row of crow- step crenellation
Example: The Street of Facades

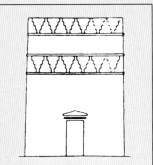

Denomination: Assyrian
Phase: II
Dates: 3rd, 2nd and 1st centuries BC
Characteristics: Two rows of crow-step crenellation
Example: The Street of Facades

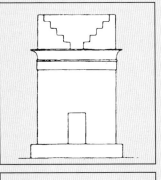

Denomination: Cavetto
Phase: I
Dates: 2nd and 1st centuries BC; 1st century AD
Characteristics: Presence of a very marked architrave called cavetto. Only one single step. No semi-columns on the facade.
Example: The Tomb of Uneishu

Denomination: Cavetto
Phase: II
Dates: 2nd and 1st centuries BC; 1st century AD
Characteristics: As per Phase I with the addition of semi-columns on the facade.

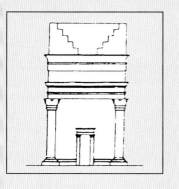

Denomination: Double Cornice
Phase: I
Dates: 1st Century BC; 1st and 2nd Centuries AD
Characteristics: Presence of a second horizontal architrave under the cavetto.
Examples: Certain tombs in the Wadi Farasa

Denomination Double Cornice
Phase: Intermediate
Characteristics: Presence of capitals between the cavetto and the underlying architrave.
Examples: The tombs at Jabal Mughar al-Nasara

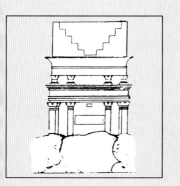

Denomination: Double Cornice
Phase: II
Characteristics: Double columns on the external corners
Examples: Turkmaniyeh, Silk and Urn Tombs

Denomination: Nabataean
Dates: 1st and 2nd century AD
Examples: Al-Khasneh, Renaissance, Broken Pediment, Sextus Florentinus, Palace, ed-Deir, and Corinthian Tombs and the Bab es-Siq Triclinium

Denomination: Roman
Dates: 2nd and 3rd centuries AD
Characteristics: Classical lines which semicircular elements substituting the tympanum
Examples: The Street of Facades, The tombs of Wadi Thughra

A path carved along the Wadi al-Mahfur leads to the High Place of Sacrifice.

Religion

In the Nabataean civilisation we find, as in every civilisation, great respect for the world of the gods, together with a profound devotion, evidenced by the large number of places of worship and burial monuments.

In the pre-Islamic tradition of Arabia, there were a number of statues or simple stones which were gathered at the Ka'aba in Mecca. These objects were considered to be either the "homes" of individual deities, or an indication of their presence, or even, to true believers, the gods themselves. The Nabataeans' most important god, too, "lived" in rock - in fact he was rock. His original name is unknown but he was later known as Dhushara, or Dushrat (Dusares, in Greek) which means "Lord of the Shara". Shara is used as a name for the chain of mountains that runs from central Edom to the Gulf of Aqaba, and includes Petra.

In the later period of their "Caravan State", other, foreign gods were added to the Nabataeans' pantheon - from ancient oriental cults, from the Greeks and from ancient southern Arabia. It is also presumed that the Nabataeans worshipped female divinities, in the tradition of all other pre-Islamic Arabian peoples. Later they worshipped the Arab goddess Allat (identified with Aphrodite, Athena and also Atargatis), Al-Uzza (Aphrodite/Venus), together with Manat or Manawat (Tyche and Nemesis), and also the goddess Isis.

In many parts of Petra there are flat niches carved in the rock from which rectangular stele emerge. These are known as beth-els or baityloi, a term which has its origin in the Aramaic expression "Beth-El", or House of God. They presumably represent the basic idol of Nabataean religion, the God of Rock - Dhushara. There are also some double bethels which may show a pair of gods, probably Dhushara and Allat together.

Similar to the bethels are the so-called "nephesh". These are pointed pillars, often drawn on the rock with large strokes, but often, as with the bethels, situated in niches.

The Nabataeo-Aramaic term nephesh means "soul", and therefore these carvings may serve in remembering the dead.

Al-Thugra (The Snake Monument)

To the south-west, there is a small necropolis of rock tombs, the most famous of which is the Snake Monument. The coiled body of the snake rests on a block of rock, with the beast's wide head pointing towards south-west. In Greek and Roman symbology, the snake had an apotropaic function, that is it was believed to ward off evil. In the case of Petra therefore, the tombs were protected in this way, however, in Nabataean tradition, the serpent is a symbol of eternity.

Jabal Harun

To reach Jabal Harun, you must pass along the Wadi Ras-Suleiman south-west of Petra, beyond the Snake Monument, through an impervious and difficult-to-reach area. At the summit of the mountain there is a small white building which is the Sanctuary of Aaron (Harun), the brother of Moses. This tiny mosque, which can be seen from a distance, is supposed to have been built over the grave of Aaron. This is the highest point in the region and from here you can enjoy the incredible scenery.

The High Place (Al-Madhbah)

At the top of Jabal al-Najr, 1,035 metres above sea-level and 190 metres above the lowest point of the city is the High Place, known in Arabic as Al-Madhbah.
It was a place of religious celebration.
The view from this holy place is marvellous and you can see right across the valley of Petra, where some scenes from the Steven Spielberg film "Indiana Jones and the Last Crusade" were shot.
On the far side you can also see the Umm al-Biyarah mountain, thought to be the biblical Selah. Further to the left there is Jabal Harun with the dome of Aaron's Grave. Although the Al-Madhbah is attributed to the Nabataeans, there are also indications that the area had a similar use in the time of the Edomites.
The High Place consists of a central courtyard of about 64 metres by 20, with two altars and drains for the blood of sacrificed animals. There is a circular platform with a ritual bath and drain and also a cistern with drain. The channels and baths served in the rites of purification.
The altar is oriented to the west, a fact which is thought to be of some religious significance, and its extraordinary position in this mountainous zone could be related to the Nabataean cult of the sun-god, which Strabo refers to in his "Geographica", Book 16, 783/784 - "[The Nabataeans] worship the sun and keep an altar at home where every day they leave offerings of drinks and smoke."

Divinities

Allat: literally, "goddess"; identified with Aphrodite and Athena

Al-Uzza: means "the powerful"; identified with Aphrodite/Venus

Atargatis: Arab goddess who protects fertility

Dhushara: principal god of the Nabataeans

Manat or Manaw: an Arab god identified with Tyche and Nemesis

Obelisk Area

To reach this area of obelisks, you turn left about 300 metres after the Al-Khasneh, where a path carved from the rock brings you across a small gorge to a low saddleback ridge. Then following a series of square, blue signposts which lead to a ridge called Zibb Attouf, which possibly translates as "merciful phallus".

Once there you will see two monolithic obelisks, more than 6 metres in height and about 30 metres apart. They were carved out of the rock, levelling the summit of the mountain.

According to Iain Browning, they probably represent Nabataean deities, like Dhushara or Al-Uzza. However, Dhushara was never venerated in the form of an obelisk, usually represented as a block or a block relief.

The Nabataean obelisks with their nephesh, or images in relief, symbolise the souls of the dead.

The Lion Fountain

The Lion Fountain is situated south of the outer Siq, between the Garden Tomb and the area of obelisks. From the High Place, you descend a flight of steps cut from the rock in the direction of Wadi Farasa, which lead to the Lion Fountain.

The Garden Tomb (Next page)

Not far from the High Place of Sacrifice and very close to the Lion Fountain lies the Garden Tomb, also known as the Garden Temple. In a beautiful reconstruction by W. Bachmann in 1917, the grandeur of this Hellenistic monument can be clearly seen. It is thought to date back to the reign of Harith IV (9 BC - 40 AD). Beside and to the right of the main building, which has a facade with two columns and two angular pillars, there are some steps which lead to a terrace with a triclinium and a large bath.

The Tomb of the Roman Soldier

Coming from the Garden Tomb, you arrive at the Tomb of the Roman Soldier. It has an ornate facade with three statues dressed as Roman legionaries. The central door of the tomb is decorated with columns which support the trabeation, or horizontal beams, and the tympanum. The mausoleum is in the Hellenistic style.

The Triclinium (Next page)

Opposite the Tomb of the Roman Soldier there is a Triclinium, or sacred hall. It is a sepulchral monument with fluted half-columns which alternate with niches, and are thought to form part of a complex together with the Roman Soldier's tomb. It is a large hall carved out of the rock and has wonderful colouring - rose, purple and orange - and would have been used to hold sumptuous funeral banquets in honour of the antecedents of the family who owned the mausoleum of the Roman Soldier.

The Renaissance Tomb

Following the gorge along the Wadi Farasa, passing other rock monuments, you reach the Renaissance Tomb, whose name derives from the fact that its design reflects the pure architectural lines of the Renaissance Period. The elegant entrance is crowned by an arch with two columns which support a double trabeation and pediment.

The Broken Pediment Tomb

Near the Renaissance Tomb lies the Broken Pediment Tomb. Its facade is in the Nabataean style, with simple, elegant lines. The tomb probably belonged to an influential Nabataean family.

Hydraulic Engineering

The way of life of nomads, as the Nabataeans were at the beginning of their history, required a well-defined organisation and a rational adaptation of the structure of the land and the climatic conditions.

Used to adapting, and once finally able to locate a zone which filled their needs, the Nabataeans set about demonstrating their capacity for inventiveness, which manifested itself not only in the construction of rock buildings but also in their hydraulic engineering. The great models of irrigation systems of the southern Arabs, like the dam at Marib (in present-day Yemen) or those of Mesopotamia and Egypt, would surely have driven the Nabataeans to build their own system. In fact, they built many cisterns, canals, dams and aqueducts, underwater pipes and pipes in the rock throughout their territory.

The dam built at the entrance to the Siq merits special attention after the disastrous damage caused by floods.

The Nabataeans were also lucky to have found water in the area of Petra, thanks to the peculiarities of the terrain - its granite base stops the water from penetrating too deeply, forcing it to remain near the surface, and making it easier to use.

On these pages, some views of Petra in landscapes drawn by David Roberts.

48

Urn Tomb

The strongest visual impact of the twelve mausoleums is made by the Urn Tomb, so called because of the urn crowning the building, which has erroneously been called a courthouse. The imposing facade, which is extremely high, has four columns which support the trabeation, surmounted by a second trabeation, an attic and a pediment. The central tomb perhaps belonged to King Malik II (40 - 70 AD). A Greek inscription states that the building was consecrated as the "cathedral" of Petra in the year 446 AD.

Silk Tomb

Near the Urn Tomb we find the Silk Tomb, also known as the "Rainbow Tomb" because of the multicoloured striations in the sandstone of its facade. The colours range from white to blue, from salmon pink to grey and vivid red. You can also see a flight of Assyrian-type steps, although they are rather badly damaged.

Corinthian Tomb

Beside the Palace Tomb there is the Corinthian Tomb, which is unfortunately in a very dilapidated condition.
This two-level monument shows a mixture of architectural styles. The capitals which lent their name to the monument, are not in fact in the Corinthian style, but are instead in a floral Nabataean style.

Palace Tomb

This building, which lies beside the Corinthian Tomb, has all the appearances of a Palace as a result of its imposing size. Although the facade is quite badly damaged, it is still possible to make out clearly three levels, surmounted by columns and pillars side by side.

On pages 56 and 57, panoramic view of the necropolis of Mughar al-Nasara.

Tomb of Sextus Florentinus

The last tomb to the north of the so-called "royal wall", is the mausoleum of Sextus Florentinus who was a governor of the Province Arabia under the Emperor Hadrian. It is the only tomb which bears an inscription, in Latin, from which the monument can be dated to around 130 AD. We also learn from the inscription that the tomb was donated by Lucius, the son of Sextus Florentinus.

Turkmaniyeh Tomb

Having passed by the ruins of a circular tower of Roman times which was once part of the Nabataean walls, north of Petra, you arrive at the Turkmaniyeh Tomb in the Wadi Abu' Ullaqa. Only the upper portion of the facade remains today - the lower part is missing. This tomb is important above all for its five-line inscription in Nabataean, dating from halfway through the 1st century AD, which is situated between the inner semi-columns of the stone facade. It is an interesting epitaph as it places under the protection of the god Dhushara not only the mausoleum with its stone rooms, but also "the courtyard in front of the tomb ... the gardens and the triclinium, the water cisterns, the terraces and the walls" and prohibits the removal of any object from the tomb. The inscription also permits the burial of other bodies in the tomb in the presence of a written contract. This monument teaches us about the inhabitants religious values (the inviolability of the tomb) and also about the religious regulation (binding contracts for places in these stone mausoleums).

Another important piece of information gleaned from the inscription is an indication of the function of the various elements of Nabataean tombs - they are part of a religious complex including banqueting halls for the funeral ceremonies, reservoirs for water and so on.

On the next page, the colonnaded street which led to the centre of the lower city.

The Temenos

In the heart of Petra, in the lower city, there is a sacred area known as the Temenos.
The Monumental Gate of the Temenos, with its three arches, bordered the colonnaded road in its entire width and marked the dividing point between the sacred area and the profane area. It was constructed in honour of the Emperor Trajan in 114 AD, and would originally have held a wooden door, and have served as a triumphal arch and doorway to the Temenos.

Excavation work has revealed many fragments of sculptures, columns and bas-reliefs of various types. On the southern side of the Temenos there are the remains of a staircase, a small bath, a triclinium, some statue bases and a door inscribed to King Harith IV (9 BC - 40 AD). An altar was also discovered, which turned out to be the altar from the temple to Dhushara.

Qasr al-Bint Farun Temple

On the western side of the Temenos is the Qasr al-Bint Farun, whose name given to it by the Bedouins means "the Castle of the Pharaoh's Daughter". The temple, whose walls are about 32 metres high, is constructed from stone blocks and not carved from the rock. It is the best preserved Nabataean building and probably dates to the 1st century BC. It was dedicated to Dhushara, the principal divinity in the Nabataean pantheon.

The Petra Museum

The ancient museum of Petra is found to the north-west in the lower city near the northern walls. It is situated in a cave which used to be a Nabataean tomb, and due to its multicoloured appearance was originally called the Rainbow Temple.

On these pages, some different views of the Petra Museum.

Writing and Language

The Greek historian Diodorus Siculus, who lived at the time of Julius Caesar and Augustus, quotes as his source Jeronymus of Cardia (360 - 260 BC) when he tells that the Nabataeans used Aramaic, a Syrian and therefore Semitic language. The first historical document, from 312 BC, is in fact in Aramaic. It is a letter of reconciliation sent by the diadochus Antigonos Monophthalmos (381 - 301 BC) following a nocturnal attack on the Nabataeans. It was as a result of the military campaigns of Alexander the Great that Greek became widespread throughout the Near East. Greek became the language of government and of trade. It was to be found on the coins of the Egyptian Ptolomeys and the Seleucid kings of Syria, which were also legal tender in Jordan. Greek is also the most important language of Christianity in Jordan, but despite this, once the Romans had conquered the area, Latin became widespread and is found in inscriptions on monuments, on Imperial dedications, military reports, road signs and funerary inscriptions. The most important monument in Jordan with a Latin inscription is the rock tomb of Sextus Florentinus, the Roman Legate to Arabia, who died in Petra in the year 140 AD.

The language of the Nabataeans was, however, Aramaic. With its 22 consonants which derive from the Phoenician alphabet, this language became ever more important in the Near East, replacing the more complex cuneiform writing. The paucity in Nabataean inscriptions can be explained by the lifestyle of the Nabataeans, who were essentially nomads, but also by the type of trade which they engaged in, which in the 4th, 3rd and 2nd centuries BC was principally a form of barter.

Only in the 1st century BC, when Petra became commercially important and an autonomous political entity, did the Arab "cultural void" come to an end. The Nabataeans began to mint coins with names inscribed, and inscriptions started to appear on monuments, in a style which, though modelled on Greek and Roman forms, was unmistakably Nabataean. The most important example comes from the Turkmaniyeh Tomb which dates to halfway through the 1st century BC, with an inscription to the god Dhushara. In one way has Nabataean writing reached our times - it is the basis for modern Arabic writing.

The Nabataean Museum

A new museum has been founded in a building adjacent to a modern restaurant. Displayed here are various examples of Nabataean pottery, including some figures in terracotta which represent camels and other animals. There are also some copies of Greek statues together with jewellery, coins, high-relief carvings, lamps and glasswork.

Valuable finds on display in the Nabataean Museum.

The Lion Tomb, or Triclinium

Along the road to ed-Deir, after a pleasant walk through imposing ravines and pathways cut along cliff edges, you arrive at a small gorge which leads to the Lion Tomb. The facade of this monument is one of the most classical of all Nabataean structures. There are two relief lions carved in the rock in heraldic position at the entrance to the hypogeum, one opposite the other. In Nabataean religion, lions are associated with certain ancient Middle Eastern gods.

On the previous page, the path which leads to the Lion Tomb and the Ed-Deir, shown on the following pages.

Ed-Deir
(The Monastery)

Lying far from the other monuments, carved in the rock in an opening to the north-west of Petra, is the so-called monastery, Ed-Deir in Arabic. It is by far the largest of Petra's tombs, being 40 metres high, including the urn which is 9 m high, and 47 metres across. As it is situated on a high plain, it offers a marvellous view which extends as far as Wadi Arabah, 1,500 metres below, which runs along the Israeli-Jordanian border from the shores of the Dead Sea down to the Red Sea. Towards the south-west you can spot the little white mosque on the summit of Jabal Harun, where Moses' brother Aaron lies. In the five niches of the Ed-Deir facade there were once statues, but as to whether they were images of famous dead personages, or Nabataean divinities, we do not yet know. A Nabataean votive inscription near the stone building mentions the venerated king Aboud III (30 - 9 BC) whose tomb is held to be in the ruined Israeli town of Avdat in the Negev desert, a city which was founded by this king. As indicated in a "chapel" in the Wadi Nmeir, near the Wadi Farasa, King Aboud, or Obodas, was venerated in Petra after his death. The Ed-Deir could therefore be a posthumous sanctuary dedicated to Aboud, who may be the figure represented in the central niche of the upper level. Archaeological studies have excluded the theory that this was a mausoleum, as the room, 12 x 11 m, carved out of the rock inside the building contains no buried tombs nor wall niches for burial.

Coins

The life of the Nabataeans between the 4th and the first half of the 2nd centuries BC, is still more or less unknown and many questions have yet to be answered. As trade was originally based on a barter system, the appearance of coinage was later here than in other places. Only much later, when Nabataea became a political power, did coins begin to be produced in silver and bronze. Various Nabataean kings appear on the coinage, for example Malik I (60 - 30 BC) and Harith IV (9 BC - 40 AD).

Pottery

Nothing remains today of the nomadic period of Nabataea. No inscriptions, no coins, no pottery. The few examples of Hellenistic art found at Petra were imported, as at other centres in the Negev like Loz, Nizzana and Avdat. The Nabataeans only started producing pottery themselves in the 1st century BC.
Three different excavation sites in Petra have produced examples of Nabataean pottery - at the Siq, the Qasr al-Bint Farun and at the Zurrabeh ceramics complex near the Petra Forum Hotel. Some Roman and Byzantine material has also been found. The design of fine first phase Nabataean pots bears many resemblances to Hellenistic pottery design, that is to say flowers and leaves on pink terracotta, but they soon developed into a more individual style.
Pomegranates feature heavily in Nabataean pottery.

Local Crafts

Petra is home to a very original craft - coloured sand. It is taken from the rocks at Petra and bottled in varying forms and sizes.

Some of the local crafts, handed down from ancient techniques and traditions.

Some characteristic views of the Nabataean city today.

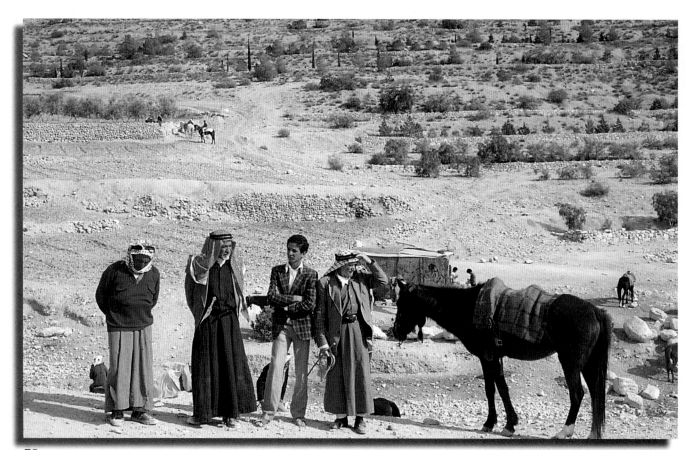

Breadmaking today can evoke the movements and methods of past millenia.

Spinning wool is still an occupation reserved for the women.

Siq al-Barid

At a distance of about 6 km north of the centre of Petra, there is a small gorge called as-Siq al-Barid which leads to a small Nabataean centre known as "Little Petra" where there are also buildings carved out of the rock.

This was an important commercial suburb of the Nabataean capital and was used as a base for foreign trade. The land was cultivated in terraces and in fact still is today. Apart from the monumental tombs, the irrigation system is in a good state of repair. The rock buildings of the as-Siq al-Barid have a preponderance of religious sites, among which are four large triclinia. Inside the gorge there is a stairway cut into the rock which leads to a room of about 5 m in height which was possibly a biklinium for worshipping. The room contains frescoes on the ceiling which are a rare surviving example of Nabataean painting.

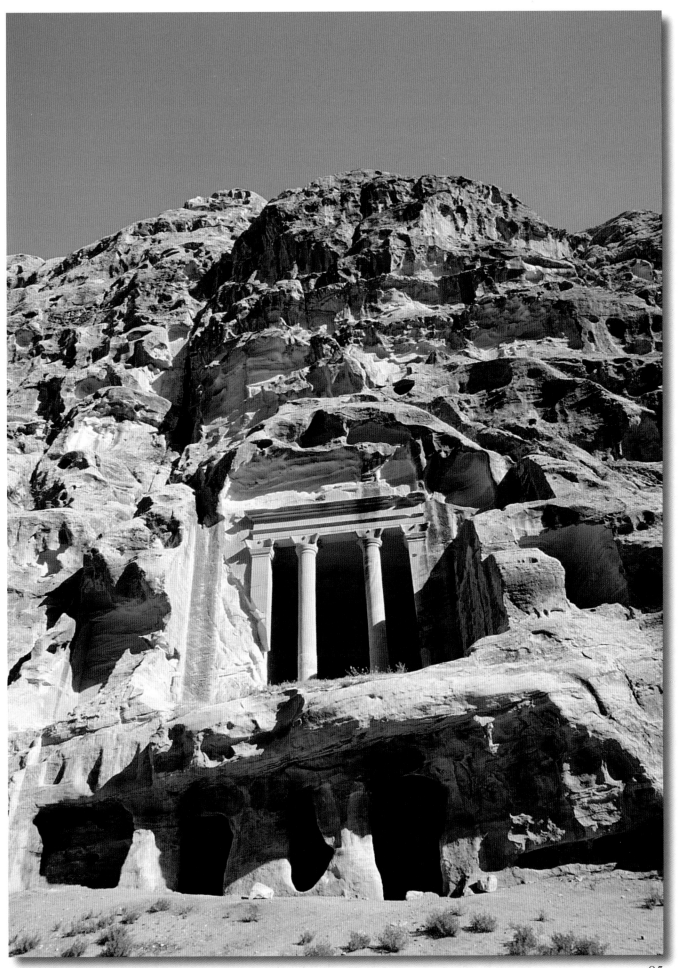

Al-Baidha

The neolithic settlement of al-Baidha, or el-Beida, is of enormous archaeological interest. It lies north of Petra, 1 km south of the as-Siq al-Barid, and is thought to be one of the oldest cities in the Middle East.

In 1956 a Bedouin brought the British archaeologist Diana Kirkbride to the site and in 1958 the excavation work began. Throughout the various period of work six levels of Neolithic dwellings were discovered, covering the period between 7000 and 6500 BC. The order of the layers begins with circular houses joined together, and finishes with separate rectangular dwellings. Kirkbride also discovered, about 50 m east of the houses and workshops, some of which may even have been two-storey buildings, something rather interesting - a series of circular walls with flat paved floors, possibly "caskets" in a sacred area.

Outside the urban area there has also been found a necropolis which reveals practically identical funerary practices as at Jericho.

The Royal Tombs

North-west of the Wadi Musa in the centre of Petra there rises a sandstone mountain which forms part of Jabal al-Khubtha. On the side which faces towards Petra a number of tombs, usually known as the Royal Tombs, were carved. It is a collection of imposing facades, some of which are over 30 metres high. It is presumed that these monuments, which include the Urn Tomb, the Corinthian Tomb, the Palace Tomb, the Silk Tomb and the tomb of the Roman Proconsul Sextus Florentinus, were the mausoleums of Nabataean kings. They are held to have been built between the 1st and 2nd centuries AD.

The Rock Structure

The visitor to Petra is always struck by the shapes and extraordinary colours of the sandstone there. This phenomenon of holed rocks, shaped stones, vertical cliffs and huge cracks, is the work of earthquakes, water flows and weather conditions which have all left their mark on the features of Petra over millions of centuries.

The sandstone is a multitude of colour due to the effect of various metallic oxides, while the unusual shapes which almost seem like the grain in wood, is an effect of seismic activity in the area.

While nature's little joke seems to have been appreciated in the majority of the monuments, many of the so-called royal tombs are without this rich design, having been covered with a uniformly beige plaster.

Glossary

Acroter: from the Greek "upper part": elements which adorn the top and the corners of the pediment

Agora: meeting place and market

Apotropeic: which wards off evil

Attic: in Petra means a low level between the trabeation and the end of the facade

Beth-El: from the Greek "baitylos" and Aramaic "beth-'el", "house of God": stelae or simple rocks or sculptures used as objects of worship

Biklinium: banqueting hall for use during sacrifices or remembrance services; contains benches on either side of the room for resting during the meal

Cardo: main street in military camps and Roman towns running north/south

Cavea: spectator area in a theatre

Cell: closed room used for purposes of worship in a temple whose only light comes from the entrance

Decumanus: important road running east/west which intersects the Cardo

Jinn-block: stone block which popular belief holds to contain the souls of the dead

Diadochus: from Greek, meaning "successor": they were the generals of Alexander the Great, who divided up his empire between them upon his death in 323 BC

Jabal: Arabic word meaning "mountain"

Hypogeum: underground construction usually used for burial

Mensa sacra: altar

Nephesh: Nabataean sculpture: representation of an obelisk carved in relief on the rock in memory of a dead person, similar to the bethel; sometimes found carved into a niche in the rock

Nymphaeum: sanctuary of the Nymphs in Ancient Greece; in modern architecture it is used to indicate fountains of particular architectural or urbanistic interest

Pantheon: temple dedicated to all the gods

Portico: ground-level construction with a covering supported by columns or pillars

Tholos: round temple with a truncated conical structure

Tympanum: triangular central part of pediment, between horizontal trabeation and sloping frames of pediment

Trabeation: (on a facade) the part of the architrave, frieze and cornice which rests on columns

Triclinium: sacred or commemorative banquet hall for the dead; with benches on three sides of the room

Wadi: valley or dry river bed

Index

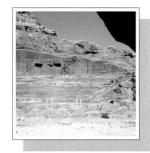